The Confessions of a Sex Addict
Part I

The Confessions of a Sex Addict

Part I

Michael Wynne

Kiss and Tell Press, London

Kiss and Tell Press
theconfessionsofasexaddict.com

First published in 2011
copyright © 2011 by Michael Wynne

ISBN 978-1-4710-6672-6

I have to be careful what I say... But it's hard. Impromptu confession can be as irresistible as sex.

Andrea Lee, *Interesting Women*

1. The Colombian Guy

This Columbian guy comes over, a bit younger than me, all smooth and brown and compact, a mix of Turkish, Welsh and native Indian, that typical fusion you find in South America, or the Caribbean. So he comes over and he wants to be fucked. He'd made this clear while we chatted online. I'll be the hairy older guy and he'll be the short slim one. The dynamic almost goes without saying, though by the time we've come and are lying there in bed, he says my arse is too good not to fuck and that next time he'll be doing the fucking.

"I only get fucked about once every two years," I tell Ricardo the Columbian, which is true, and not because I don't like it or because I'm some big fucking top, it's just that I don't often meet guys who want to fuck someone bigger than them. (Let's never forget the skinny Catalan rock star who, a few months ago, was very eager to do the fucking, and he did it well.)

Ricardo's a good kisser and he has this way of kissing that's to put his tongue deep in your mouth to let you know he wants it sucked. His lips are soft. His whole mouth is soft, which is apparent, too, when he puts my cock in it. My cock is not small, but he makes it feel as manageable as a chipolata... which isn't a sexy thought, but it's the first thing that comes to mind. A bit like that moment in David Leavitt's story "The Term-Paper Artist" when the young Jewish guy pulls down his tracksuit bottoms and his dick sits there, Leavitt says, like a sausage on a mound of black beans.

The strength of Ricardo's suction makes fucking his mouth impossible; he decides when the cock goes in and out. I feel trapped, slightly anxious he'll bite my dick off. His arse is a different matter. My cock slides in with ease; there'd even been a moment before we started fucking when he was sitting on my middle and I was rubbing my cock against his crack and it slid in. Just a couple of seconds, before I realised what was happening.

"That's crazy," I said, and pulled it out.

He says he's never had someone put their tongue in his nostril, never had someone slap his face while they're fucking him, never told anyone his boyfriend's name, not even his regular fuck-buddies (a dentist and a graphic designer). He hasn't told either of them that his boyfriend's coming over from Berlin for a few days. I'm the only one who knows about Dieter. Ricardo has told the other two that he's going away for a week to see his cousins in Spain, so that him and his boyfriend can spend a long weekend together. Then Dieter will go back to Berlin and Ricardo will stay in London to finish his English course. We agree there'll be a next time.

"I'm coming back for your arse," he says.

But he never does.

2. We're Splitting Up

A couple of weeks ago, my own boyfriend and I split up. Things weren't working out. It's a relief. We weren't together for that long, just a couple of months, but we were trying out the whole monogamy thing which I realised from early on was not for me. Despite him having a great arse and the kind of body I like – all tall and slim – the sex between us wasn't that great. I don't think he was really into sex. A lot of English guys aren't. They like to suck cock and they like to get fucked and they'll play with your tits if you ask them, but they don't know how to spend hours having sex, like sucking and licking and exploring the body with their hands and tongue and skin.

I'm sounding like a romantic.

Maybe I am.

I love sex and I like a lot of it and I like to get into the whole body of someone, not just his arsehole and his mouth. Kissing and fucking is great, but there's more to sex than that. Even in the sauna I need that, even in a sex club. The best sex in places like that is when you come across a guy who's really into men's bodies, and they want to stick their tongue everywhere, and nothing disgusts them. They're happy to follow their nose. Those are the guys who are so pleased not to be in the closet anymore that they'll go out and do what they've always wanted to do, or they're the kind of guy who is so desperate for sex, so starved for the touch of another man – they're often married or have girlfriends – that they really just want to hold you or be held by you so that they can breathe in your smell.

I must have been about five years old when I started falling in love with my classmates and staring at the chests of their fathers, waiting for that moment when the gym teacher would tell us to hit the showers, that delicious mixture of embarrassment and lust. That's the smell I want when I have sex, the sweetness of locker rooms and sweaty crevices. I used to date this guy who insisted I brush my teeth after rimming him. He loved being rimmed, but the thought of kissing me afterwards, with maybe a bit of his own stink on my breath, disgusted him.

My boyfriend wasn't like that – he had other issues – but when it came to the kinky bits, he was up for it. He liked being spat on, particularly on his chest, and then wiping my spit across his nipples and saying thank you. From the start I knew it wasn't going to work, despite the things we had in common – we liked going to the cinema together, we jogged in the park together, we sat in cafes and people-watched, we drank coffee (espresso for me; lattes for him).

There is a part of me that wants the domestic thing. But there are other parts, too.

3. The Warm Heart

This Nigerian guy, Adrian, arrives at my place expecting a bath with bubbles, candles and the new Dwele CD. It's what I'd promised him. I run the bath when he gets here, drizzling Radox Mimosa Bath Foam into the water, scattering it with my hand, back and forth, frothing it with the tips of my fingers on the surface of the water, which, he says, is exactly how his mother used to do it when he was a kid. He'd been speaking to her on the phone while we chatted online.

He smells of Jill Saunders aftershave and Sure deodorant, of sweet white bread. His arsehole, after a quick bath, lying on his back on my bed with his legs in the air, tastes of Lux Beauty Soap. He wants to pause, says he wants to get to know me, so we sit naked, cross-legged, smoking a spliff, my first in years, the smoke sharp against the back of my throat.

"Men," he says, as if this is what we've been talking about. "They always lie and cheat."

"Who said that?" I say.

"Me," he says. "It's true. Men lie."

"No, they don't," I say.

"Yes, they do."

"They only lie if you let them," I say.

He strokes my head until he gets to the scar on my temple.

"An accident," I say. "When I was four. My mother drove her Mini into an ambulance."

"And what happened?"

"Twenty-nine stitches," I say. "My head was split open and my brain was hanging out."

"Was it?" he says.

"No," I say.

"You lied to me," he says, turning away, burying his head in the pillow.

"You're a drama queen," I say.

"I get it from my mother," he says, peering up at me, a kid who'd rather talk than sulk. "If I came home late at night, she wouldn't speak to me for days. I was seventeen and getting fucked by this white guy from Yorkshire. He was married. My mother was weird. When we were kids we had two of everything – trousers, shirts, socks, underpants – one for the wash and one to wear."

With the perfect soundtrack any moment can be beautiful.

Norah Jones sings "One Flight Down" while Adrian tells me how his father used to beat him: "I'll beat you until your nose bleeds," he used to say.

"And what did you do?" I say.

"I just said, yeah, whatever."

"Oh," I say.

"He's gone now," he says.

I take his hand and we stand up to dance, arms at our sides, barely touching, chest to chest, our cocks hard, our thighs tickling each other's. We sway in slow motion, as slow as Norah Jones' "Nightingale" dictates.

Splinters of light frame the window blind. We stroke each other's backs and arses, so gently, as if any pressure could bruise the skin. He rests his head on my shoulder. The higher we get, the harder it is to distinguish his body from mine. We're weightless, our bodies snakes in a pit, slithering over and through each other. We behave like lovers, like this is the beginning of something.

We sleep close together, on our stomachs, his leg heavy on my thigh. As I'm drifting off, I wonder if the weight of his leg could stop the blood from getting to my feet. He is 6'3", from healthy Nigerian stock. I think how you were so light compared to him, in colour and mass, that maybe I was just too heavy for you.

"Am I squashing you?" I'd say after sex, lying on your chest.

"No," you'd say. "You're just warming my heart."

You being the boyfriend who just left.

4. Flicking Shit at Strangers

There's this guy I have phone sex with who's really into shit. We talk about how we'll go cruising in his car at night and show our shitholes to people and dig the doodoo out of each other's cracks and flick it at joggers, especially joggers. We'll flick shit at joggers in the park. And also at sluts, at sluts and cunts walking down the street, we'll put shit in our mouths and force them to kiss us. We'll pull down their skirts and piss on their backsides. That's what he calls it, a backside. He likes the idea of driving around after dark and going into parks and forcing guys to eat our shit. He says things like: "I'm going to squat over his face and take a dump into his mouth and then sit on him and really push down hard so he'll have to eat my shit and choke." We speak like this for about twenty minutes, sometimes more, going back and forth, his message then my message, him, then me, and I'm all the time jerking my cock, loving the feeling of my cock so hard and him and me, two men with hairy shitholes driving round and causing trouble. His voice is deep and smoky and completely fucking perverted, depraved, and his mind, too, and the way he comes up with all these ideas for things we could do with our shit.

He's not the only guy I speak to about this stuff. There's another guy on the chat-line who's into shit – he calls it pooh. We talk mainly about me fucking him, or shoving my hand up his arse. He'll say things like: Help me get this pooh out, man.

If I had the courage, if I was really as twisted and fucked-up as all that, if I was into shit in real life the way I am in my head, then... well, I guess I'd be able to find someone to do it with. Or would I? Statistically speaking, it's probably easier to find a boyfriend than to find a guy who's genuinely into shit.

5. Nobody Goes to Haiti

In a short piece she wrote for *The New Yorker*, Edwidge Danticat talks about her cousin Maxo who died in the earthquake three weeks ago, one of the tens of thousands – *hundreds* of thousands! – crushed and trapped under the rubble of Jacmel and Port-au-Prince and Léogâne, some of them flattened by the UN building or the Presidential Palace.

The earthquake came too late for Christmas, the earth's timing out of synch with the season of giving, not like it had been in 2004, for example. Then it was like whatever loose change we had, and more, we gave to Sri Lanka. These new pictures are too much like Africa, as if we've seen this all before, over and over, too many times. We've all been on holiday to Sri Lanka, but nobody goes to Haiti. Nobody cares about Africa. Edwidge doesn't say all this – it's just me and my friend McKenzie who are raging about Europe, and France in particular. McKenzie reminds us on her Facebook wall about the billions of dollars Haiti gave France two hundred years ago, pretty much at gunpoint, compensation for the loss of its slaves. The sapping of Haiti started a while back! If we didn't have to leave our rooms to eat or work – McKenzie and I teach at the same language school – these truths would be too fucking unbearable to hold onto.

Edwidge writes about her cousin Maxo's kindness, recounts how he'd often call friends and relatives in the States for help in re-building a school, or for cash to buy a coffin to bury a neighbour, or for food to give prisoners in the local jail. When they eventually found Maxo's body, dug out from under four storeys of concrete – "at least he would not rest permanently in the rubble" – Edwidge got a call from her tall beautiful cousin, the one they nicknamed Naomi Campbell, to tell of the sad news.

"Don't cry," she reassured Edwidge. "That is life."

C'est la vie. Just a short moment.

I'd come across the essay by chance, clicking from link to link, or maybe McKenzie had put it up on Facebook. I've always liked Edwidge Danticat's work. Her story "Water Child" is one of the few that haunt me, one of those stories that, on some level, feel like a metaphor for my own. A young woman, a nurse in New York, with ageing parents in Haiti, is mourning the death of her unborn baby. The father – husband to another woman. The story is told with the clarity of grief, a sadness too exhausted for invention.

The day after the disaster, Teddy Prendergrass dies of colon cancer, so every now and then someone puts up a link to "Turn Off the Lights", his voice soothing. We keep moving between tragedy and the urges of the body, manoeuvring between earthquakes and dinner, bombings and fucking. It makes me think of that day – *is it three years already?* – when the explosions went off in London.

6. The London Bombings

I'd been working at home, preparing a class (I'd only started teaching at City College International, CCI!) when a friend called to see if I was okay, which is when I first heard the news, two hours after it had happened. I stood at my window above Blackstock

15

Road – the buses had stopped, people were walking in their suits and smart skirts, mainly northwards, away from the City. I felt compelled to leave my flat, to see what London looked like on such a day. So I got on my bike and cycled up towards Islington, along Upper Street, then down City Road, onto Old Street and towards Liverpool Street Station.

One of the first things that puzzled me in this scene of empty cars passing, with just the driver inside and maybe one other person in the passenger seat, while everyone else walked home, was the lack of kinship, of social responsibility, of togetherness. In other places I've lived, drivers would have stopped, offered lifts; there wouldn't be this solemn march, pavements crowded, like a silent flocking towards a grim but important event.

The road at the top of Bishopsgate is blocked; police cars and police-people line the streets. The area has been evacuated. I don't remember my exact thinking at the time, but it felt like the right thing to do: I went to the sauna. It might have had something to do with its proximity to the no-go zone, so close to the bombs, or something about the juxtaposition of death and life. Whatever the reason, the sauna felt like the right place to be.

I remember cruising the black cubicles, round and round – there weren't many of us there – and coming across a man leaning against a wall, big and bulky and tattooed, his arms, his chest, the sides of his body, etched with intricate markings of colour: dragons, elaborate wings, roses. I followed him into a cubicle, knelt down and swallowed his cock, its shaft thick from head to base, its taste surprisingly pleasant. It's not something I do often, but at the time it was what I wanted, nothing existed but his cock. The way I was feeling then, I could have swallowed something twice the size. I kept my eyes closed and pushed my mouth onto his cock to choke myself; I wanted it as deep as it would go, past my throat, to stop me breathing, to make me gag, spit dribbling from my mouth, forcing my head onto it, like there was nothing in the world but my mouth and my breath and this thing inside me that was like blood or a hand or that moment of birth when the world opens up and you have to breathe on our own.

Someone reached into the cubicle and started playing with my nipples. I stood up and the tattoo guy knelt down and took my cock in his mouth, as if we were taking turns at this. The third guy stepped into the cubicle and stood behind me, teasing my nipples, flicking them, pressing his cock against my arse. He stroked my face, the tips of his fingers on my forehead, my cheeks, my nose, my lips, my chin, and even though his hands were calloused, his fingers dry and thick and smelling of nicotine, I welcomed it all, leaned back into him.

The tattoo guy stood up, he was taller than me, bigger. I rested my hand on the top of his arm, the ball of his shoulder, thick with muscle, and moved down to his chest, the perfect place to rest a head. He leaned in to kiss me, and the guy from behind, too. I held the tattoo guy, then turned him around to press my chest against his back; I stroked his stomach, kissed the side of his face, the back of his head. I felt cocooned in the softness between us, in this moment of extreme tenderness, so surprising yet expected, as if this was the day, if there was ever to be a day, when something like this should happen, the cosmos offering us – and if the three of us, then maybe everyone else – exactly what we needed.

I remember cycling home after that – the traffic still muted, the air thick with shock – and stopping off at Fresh and Wild in Stoke Newington for something – maybe peanut butter, maybe greens for dinner, kale, or baby spinach – and the voice over the shop's loudspeaker saying they'd be closing early to allow staff time to get home, and because of that customers could help themselves to the day's bread.

"In the spirit of giving," the voice said. "Take as many as you like."

7. Nipples

I'm 6'2" and quite muscled from the gym and years of jogging and cycling and I've got a hairy chest, though in the past few years I've started to clipper it, and because of that my pecs are more prominent. I guess you could say I have bigger than average pecs, and my nipples are a nice size, about as big as 50p coins. They are very sensitive nipples, and when I get to the point that just touching them, just brushing against them with my T-shirt, sends little shock-waves to my cock, I know it's time to get some sex.

I like to call them tits, even if most guys I have sex with call them pecs, but I like the genderfuck thing. Long ago when I used to get fucked more often, I'd ride a guy's cock and imagine my breasts banging up and down against my chest. I like to call a guy's arse his pussy. (About eighteen months ago I had sex with this guy who was into the same thing. I bought him a couple of summer frocks off eBay and I'd call him my woman. He'd say things to me, while we were fucking, like: "My man's fucking me. My man's fucking my pussy." We did this a few times, but then I wanted more and he pulled away.)

So... my nipples are at the sensitive stage – my body's telling me something! – and I'm sitting here flicking their tips as if they were my muse, as if they were the fuel to keep me writing.

If I could just carry on doing this, if I could maintain this heightened state of arousal, I'd finish a novel in a week, no problem.

But I cycle down to the sex club, which is only half-an-hour away from my flat and I pay the £5 and check my stuff in at the bar and walk around and... nothing. There aren't that many guys there and the few who are are not the kind of guy I want to have sex with. Over-weight, badly dressed, walking around with cans of beer. I'm far from picky, but since I gave up alcohol about eight years ago – mainly because I did a couple of stupid things while drunk, but really because one day I woke up in a pool of my own vomit – I've become a bit judgmental about men who drink. The smell of alcohol does not turn me on. I feel more or less the same about cigarettes.

Sex was not happening at the sex club.

It was late afternoon and my sex drive was wilting. I put my glasses back on, got my jacket from the guy behind the bar (the tall topless Eastern European guy with a smooth pumped-up chest and a gentle manner) and cycled home. I took a shower, did some sit-ups, and spent the rest of the evening on the sofa with a book about ostriches by a writer who'd grown up in the same town I had. He'd gone back to South Africa to research the ostrich trade, which my grandfather had been part of, schlepping his horse-and-cart of feathers from Outdshoorn down to the feather market in PE in the early days of the last century.

I thought about that grandfather who'd eventually left his wife and eight kids in that small town in the Cape and gone off to die in Palestine, but death took a while and he hooked up with a Polish woman, and – the story goes – spent his days hanging out on the benches of Rothschild Boulevard in Tel Aviv, playing backgammon and chess with some of the men who'd escaped Hitler's Europe.

Now I've brought the family story back to Europe, back to living amongst the white people, albeit to this strange island, a place that looks as if it could be scrunched up and slotted back into the Bay of Biscay. Or, like a wad of something coughed up out of that same maw and is now floating slowly but surely up to the North Pole.

I thought about my boyfriend, the one who was no longer my boyfriend because we'd decided it wasn't working. He'll be coming round to pick up his stuff in the next day or two... an easel, a toothbrush, some underwear, T-shirts. Maybe we could have tried harder, because when it was good it really was good. Like when we'd go jogging together in Clissold Park, our paces similar, the running smooth.

"I've never run with someone I'm dating," I said soon after we met.

"Me neither," he said, looking beautiful, as always, in his Sugoi T-shirt.

My therapist suggested recently that I'm addicted to drama and to being neurotic, that I need to learn how to share the details of my day to day with others, give credit to the mundane, make an effort to recount the every day.

"He *got* me," I said to the therapist. "He really did get me. He listened when I talked.

"And you're no big talker," he said.

"He made me *want* to talk," I said.

The strange thing is, I'm usually a good listener, but with him I wasn't that great. Maybe he was too complex, too honest. Is that how it is, is one person always the better listener? Maybe when he comes over we can watch a DVD, order a take-away from the Turkish place we like, eat on the sofa together, spoon-feed each other ice-cream straight from the tub, talk about stuff, then have sex. That was usually the setting for some of our best moments; if we could have lived on that sofa, everything would have been fine!

8. Back

I've done my back in. I went to see my chiropractor yesterday afternoon before a work meeting and he crunched my spine, then left me lying on the massage table in his therapy room in my boxers with needles in my back and upper thighs, and a single one jabbed into the top of my head. He's been fixing my back for many years now, but I was happy to see from his notes that I hadn't needed him in the past three years. The last time I'd seen him was in 2007, around the time of the bombings and The Big Break-Up.

What's three years when we're talking about loss?

McKenzie says all great loves – "like any fucking trauma" – leaves a template on our soul.

"We can never get rid of it," she says. "All we can do is learn to navigate around it."

McKenzie left her girlfriend about a year ago and hasn't dated or had sex since. She's untangling herself, she says. I say I've completely dis-entangled myself from Martin, that even when I'd bumped into him at the sauna about a year after we split up – two years ago – *and* we had sex, there was nothing there.

"I'm over him," I say.

"No such thing," McKenzie says. "You've just replaced him with Marc."

"With Marc it's just sex," I say.

"Unlikely," she says.

"And I'm over Marc, too," I say.

When Marc came round we did most of the things I'd hoped for, except watching the DVD, or having take-aways and ice-cream. I figured if I let him fuck me – which I hadn't while we were together – it would kind of make up for me dumping him, that if I let him inside me, opened up to him, laid myself bare, showed how vulnerable I could be, whatever – I'd be forgiven for instigating the end.

Which is how I did my back in.

"Stretching and heat," my chiropractor says as he removes the needles from my flesh. He's paratactic, no unnecessary words.

I react in a Pavlovian way: heat meanz steam.

So I get back on my bike, cycle from Highgate to a work meeting in the City, then a couple of hours later, head across to Waterloo, to the sauna under the arches.

It's funny how even if you're the one who initiates the split, you can still feel like you've been dumped. Part of me wanted him to beg to stay, to plead to be taken back, to try again, that sort of thing. But he didn't, and that refusal to implore felt like a type of rejection.

The guy at the sauna... his name's Jay. We've met before, about a year ago, but I decide to follow him around a bit, to feel the thrill of the hunt before going up to him. The last time was at the sauna in Vauxhall; it was my first time there, in that steamy fortress of water and shadow and light. I'd been to Tate Britain – it was the time of the Altermodern exhibition, the Triennial, and I'd wanted something a bit more corporeal, less heady, less aesthetic; the exhibition was so cerebral!

The Vauxhall sauna is built like a factory, a vast, high-ceilinged, well-kept expanse of efficiency, like it could have been an assembly plant at some point. The floors are a cream linoleum, the cubicles are immaculate, the rest-area with its sofas and televisions and coffee machines is the size of a hotel lobby. Walking around that first time, I felt like nothing but new opportunities could present themselves to me. The place felt more sex positive than the other saunas I'd been to; men stared and approached and made it known they were up for it. Or maybe it's just because they could tell I was fresh meat.

There was another first that time, something that happened with Jay, things I'd never done before.

"Gob on my face," he'd said.

We texted each other in the weeks after that, but never managed to meet up. I was the one doing the avoiding. I think the violence of our sex, or what at the time seemed violent – I'd never spat on anyone or called them a cunt, never slapped a guy – and it scared me, felt like a slippery slope.

My sexual repertoire was changing, and I panicked.

I've come a long way since then. I've ridden the slippery slope like a pro. A surfer on the slimy wave of kink.

After about ten minutes of following Jay around at the sauna in Waterloo, he and I are in a cubicle. I still haven't told him my name, nor that I recognise him from last time. He's just what I like. Not as skinny as I like, but his body is firm, so firm it's as if he's made of something harder than muscle. He's a great kisser and sucks my nipples hungrily and doesn't resist when I push him down on his knees. He gets comfortable, sits on the mattress, his back to the wall, and lets me fuck his face. These movements should be good for my back, I think, should loosen it up.

When I start playing with his arsehole he moves away from the wall and lies down on his back on the mattress. I get on top of him and we keep kissing. "What's your name?" he says. And when he tells me his, I say: "I haven't seen you in a long time." And he says: "Are you the guy from Finsbury Park?" And I say "yes", because I am.

"It's good to see you again," he says.

"You, too," I say, though we don't have much more than that to say to each other. The chemistry between us relies on actions, me in the push-up position, him on his back with his legs in the air.

9. At the Noodle Bar

Every Tuesday evening McKenzie and I go to the noodle bar in Spitalfields Market for dinner. It's near where we teach English to foreigners at City College International on Bishopsgate. We've been doing the noodle-bar thing for the past six months, from when McKenzie started working at CCI last October. We met about seven years ago when we were both involved in Queeruption, but it's only since we started going out for dinner that we've become close friends. We're similar in many ways, we seem to have similar values and similar views about what it means to be in a minority, from the colonies, living in London and trying to make art and a living.

McKenzie's Black, from the Caribbean, a dyke and a nerd. She's a painter. I'm Jewish, South African, a fag and... I'm not sure what else... a recluse, a misanthrope, a slut? I'm trying to be a writer.

The staff at the noodle bar knows us well, and seem genuinely happy to see us, and we're happy to see them, and when the ones we're used to aren't there, it takes a while for us to adjust to being served by strangers, by people who don't recognise us. We've gradually become known to most of the staff: the young Serbian woman with the dyed black hair and lip piercing; the Portuguese guy who's doing his PhD in Psychology; the cute Spaniard (he doesn't work there anymore) who introduced us to the tattoo parlour where I got my new tattoo done.

The noodle bar's part of a chain. Most dishes – maybe even all – have Japanese names, but none of the waiters or cooks or bar-staff are Japanese. We sit in a booth, if one is available, and order what we usually order: chicken katsu curry or cha han. Every now and then we'll have a yaki soba.

"So," McKenzie says. "Updates."

"There's not much to tell," I say, at which McKenzie sucks her teeth.

"The massage guy!" she says. "What about him?"

"It's just massage," I say. "No extras. Besides, he's on holiday in Italy with his folks."

"His folks!" she says. "Who the fuck goes on holiday with their mom and dad? How old's this guy?"

"He's Brazilian," I say. "He's been looking forward to it."

McKenzie and I are always famished after work, so when the food arrives we eat quickly without much talking. At some point a waiter will come and check how we're doing. *Everything okay, guys?* And if they're one of the waiters we know – the Serbian with the piercings, or the Kiwi with the dreads who does trapeze stuff at Circus Space in Hoxton. *You know Circus Space?* she says. *Sure,* I say, though I don't tell her about this guy who works there and who I see every now and then, a guy who's into fisting, who, each time I fist him, accuses me of being brutal and says we shouldn't do this anymore. The waiters will stand at our table and chat for a few minutes. McKenzie's a great listener, and the waiters tell us all sorts of things about themselves.

"She's hot," McKenzie says, when the Serbian woman's out of earshot.

"I think she'd do you," I say.

"If there's any doing to be done," McKenzie says. "I'll be doing the doing."

She's the daddy.

"Talking about little girls," I say.

"Were we?" she says.

"I was with this guy in the sauna the other day, and he got into this whole daddy scenario, even if he was about ten years older than me. But he was nice and smooth and his eyes were all puppy-dog."

I tell McKenzie how I'd spotted him in a cubicle, lying there on his back with his hands behind his head. For a moment I'd thought it was Martin – the black hair, the smooth skin, the red-brown nipples. I walked into the cubicle and touched him, the tips of my fingers on the side of his body, and when he kept still, just his eyes opening to check, then closing again, I stroked his neck, pinched his nipple, then leaned over like a flamingo to sip water, and put my lips around his tit.

"Close the door," he said.

There was no lock, so I draped my towel over the top corner of the door to secure it shut. When I turned around, he was sitting there with his cock jutting up, a considerable cock with a head like a golf ball – huge! – and in his lap, a small red First Aid kit.

"What's in your bag of tricks?" I say.

"I like getting fisted," he says.

"Oh," I say.

"It's just some gloves and stuff," he says.

He's a journalist, the UK correspondent for a Catalan daily. He's been living in Barcelona for the past twelve years, but still has a flat in Bounds Green. I like to know these things. He'd just come back from Kyrgyzstan, he tells me; they'd sent him there to cover the story of the new president.

"I'm impressed," says McKenzie.

"You should have seen his other skills," I say.

"Like a flower?" she says.

"Like a flower," I say.

Long story short: He took it all the way up to the wrist. He wanted to be my boy, for me to smack his bum the way his sports master did, to cane him.

He was demented from sniffing poppers. I bit his nipples and he sniffed; I slapped his arse until my palm burnt and he sniffed; I fisted him – three, four, five fingers – easy! – and he sniffed. The sound of my hand against his smooth arse like the crack of a whip, and the people outside in the corridor made the appropriate noises: gasps and moans of sympathy and approval.

Afterwards, he cuddled up to me – I was his daddy and he was my baby. He cried. I've been naughty, he said – planting the seeds for each step of the drama. I like the way he suddenly turned – the way he slipped and called himself daddy at some point – the way he became aggressive: *Fuck the shit out of me, you bastard*, he said. *All you fucking South Africans are the same.*

"You like that?" I said. "Big daddy fucking you."

"Yes, daddy," he said.

"You're my boy," I said. "My little pussy. My baby girl."

Suddenly he froze, became serious. "Don't tell me you're into little girls," he says. "Are you?"

McKenzie laughs.

"And I'm like: I've got a fist up your arse and you're calling me daddy, what the fuck are you talking about?"

"Jeez," McKenzie says. "Your life!" she says. "It's crazy. You should make a movie out of it."

The Portuguese waiter comes to ask if we want desserts – *I know you don't*, he says. *But I have to ask anyway. We're closing the kitchen in five minutes.* We order some green tea, another glass of water. Most of the people have gone; we're often the last people to leave. We like the noodle bar, the efficiency of it all, it's clean and at this time of the evening it's quiet, just the sound of the cooks washing up, the waiters topping up bottles of soya sauce and chilli oil. McKenzie says she's started a new canvas.

"It's a good sign," she says.

"Have you heard anything from Neeta?" I say.

"Nada," she says. "Nada from Neeta."

Which makes me think of our nada who art in nada, etc, but I don't say anything, and we walk to Bishopsgate, McKenzie to the train station, me on my bike, past the sauna, past the people sitting at tables on the pavement outside the bars in Shoreditch, up towards Finsbury Park, and home, and sleep.

10. The Walking Man

The skinny young boy in the dry sauna is definitely interested. I'm playing with my cock and he moves closer, comes over from where he's sitting by the door. He's nervous and keeps looking at the small window in the sauna door, as if someone might walk in and catch us. Oh, to be bad and to know you won't get caught! What's the worst that can happen? An over-zealous audience? Witnesses to our depravity? The sudden appearance of a familiar face? He's the kind of skinny I like, tall, sharp, just skin and bone. He touches my cock tentatively, moves his fist up and down the shaft, almost not touching; any gentler and we'd be left with only an intention, a miming gesture. The illusion of a wank.

"Do you want to suck it," I say.

"I won't, thanks," he says.

"Where you from?" I say, unable to quite place his accent, but he doesn't like being asked questions. He says it's a typical English way of interrogating people.

"I'm not English," I say.

"Who cares where I'm from?" he says.

"How old are you?" I say

"And you?" he says

"I'm thirty-five," I say.

"Me," he says. "I'm twenty-four."

His prick has the rock-hardness of youth.

"Do you want me to suck it?" I say.

"I'm not really into much," he says.

I brush the fringe away from his eyes

"Is that a yes or no?" I say.

"No, thanks," he says.

I move closer to kiss him, but he lowers his head just a fraction, demurely, and says: "Sorry." And yet he remains close, his body pressed against mine as if asking me to stay, to just be there next to him. His stomach is lovely to stroke, firm and taut, not from muscle. The thought of being inside him makes me hard. His shyness excites me, makes me think thoughts I don't want to think, a kind of insight into the appeal of innocence, the attraction of violation, the buzz of superior strength. But he is not a child.

"Your hair," he says.

"What?" I say.

"Can I touch it?" he says, and puts his hand on my chest, his eyes opening in wonder.

I smile at him. I've always felt entitled to beautiful men, that my desire for them is justification enough. And maybe because I believe this, I get them, even if it means sitting here on a ledge with a stranger whose body, from head to toe, is everything I've ever wanted.

"You've got a kind face," he says.

"Have I?" I say.

"Some people have very unkind faces."

He puts an arm around my waist, pulls himself into me, kisses my shoulder.

"I like big men," he says.

This other guy who'd been cruising me earlier – he could be Spanish – comes in and sits down next to us, starts jerking himself off. I am leaning forward with my elbows on my knees, the way butch men do, and the skinny guy takes the tip of my nipple between his fingers and plays, delicately, the way he did with my cock, and I am grateful for this, for his intuiting the gesture that brings me great pleasure. I touch his arm, then his cock. The heat is intense, like it could consume our bodies; still, my cock is hard in the Spaniard's mouth. I touch the skinny guy's shoulder and he lifts his head to look at me.

"It's too hot in here," he says.

"It's good for your skin," I say.

But he gets up anyway and strides off and out of the sauna, looking a bit like Giacometti's statue, "l'homme qui marche".

So the Spanish guy and I get down to business.

11. Sylvia Plath's Bath

Spring is in the air. The sun is out and it's almost warm, just a slight chill, which you can feel if you're on your bike, and I'm on my bike heading for the sauna in Waterloo. It's that time of year again, time for the London Lesbian and Gay Film Festival, which I am *not* going to. Still, I stop off at the Southbank for a club-sandwich, which I eat on a bench by the river, my face to the sun. For me, this is what London is about: here by the river, St Paul's to your right, Big Ben to your left, the Thames flowing before you.

The guy stands at the edge of my bench and looks down at the unoccupied end.

"Is it possible to sit here?" he says.

He's Italian, smartly dressed (cream jeans, light brown cashmere polar neck), handsome in a Parisian kind of way. There are several empty benches either side of us. I motion with my hand to imply, *sure, go ahead*, and carry on eating. A club-sandwich is always a delight; its layers and textures and flavours: soft and chewy and crunchy, the tenderness of chicken meat. When I visit my brother in New York, there's a cafe I like to go to, on the corner of Prince Street, not far from Bookworks on Crosby Street, where they serve a great club sandwich with fries. I like to sit in the room at the far end of the cafe and take my time and scribble in my notebook while families of tourists eat their lunches around me.

"Are you here for the festival?" I say.

"For holiday," he says.

"You having a good time?"

"I love London," he says.

"Are you on your own?" I say.

"Excuse me?" he says.

"Friends," I say. "Did you come with friends?"

"I come with my friend but he hate London," he says. His smile gentle; his eye-contact forthright. "He go back to Rome after two days."

"Oh," I say.

"He say everything in London is, how you say... thief. Everything they take from somewhere, from Egypt, from Asian, from Sud America."

"Yes," I say.

"I'm sorry," the guy says. "My English is not so good."

"It's fine," I say.

"Do you want to go for a coffee?" he says.

"I can't," I say.

But some people are persistent. It's not like he's not a handsome man, it's just that I've become a bit of a stranger to continuity, to sex within relating. If we're not in a cubicle or a club, it all becomes a bit more complicated.

"Maybe next time," he says. His name is Mario. "I come to London again in one week. We can meet?"

"Sure," I say, and give him my email address.

Earlier that day – clicking from link to link – I'd read something Hemingway had said, something from his Nobel speech, which the American ambassador to Sweden, or someone like that, had read out for him at the ceremony. What stayed with me were his words about the importance of being lonely, of being alone and bearing that loneliness, that in order to write you have to face, on a daily basis, the big unknown (eternity, he called it, or the lack thereof), and if you don't, well, your writing will suffer. Recognition dilutes the work.

He's right, I think. I feel most myself when I'm alone. Sylvia Plath says in *The Bell Jar* that she never feels more herself than when she's in the bath, that place where one is so purely alone. Her bath-tub is my bath-house. The sauna, more than anywhere else, is where I feel, almost always – because nowhere can be *that* reliable – completely myself, happy to be on my own, unfettered by shame and envy and disappointment. Most times when I go I feel open, confident; I can tell when I'm going to have a good time.

But there are days when you go to the sauna with a desperate need to be touched or loved, or just to have someone speak to you in this city where days can go by without a decent conversation, days without someone to hold you. At times like these, things can go either way – luck and the smell of desperation are deciding factors.

My theory: If you go to the sauna with a clear and honest idea of what you want, then you're likely to get it. Today I am going because I want to be there, to sit in a hot room with other men, naked; a men-only space where I can take my clothes off and look and be seen by men and not feel judged. I'm not particularly horny or in need of validation. All this, too, and without going into too much detail, is about women and my mistrust of them. I have been mocked by women, made to feel inadequate. Over the years, men have demonstrated a reliable degree of attention.

12. Size Matters

Later, I'm standing at one end of the upstairs cruising area, near the cleaning closet, when I notice him coming towards me. But he walks past me without a lingering glance. He's definitely the cutest guy here, about my height, but skinny, and dark – some sort of mix, maybe Brazilian, or just Spanish, his skin a soft shade of brown. I like smooth men, smooth men with slim, firm bodies.

A couple of minutes later we cross paths again and I can see he's interested, and that his interest has something to do with me being bigger than him – in bulk, not in cock-size, as I'll soon find out.

Some men love cock. A lot of men love cock. My cock is an average kind of cock, though it might be slightly thicker than average, and judging from similar ones I've encountered, it's the kind of cock that fits nicely into a mouth. Which is what this guy wanted.

We go into a cubicle, close the door, and he's on his knees, no small-talk, no foreplay; he's not even interested that the cubicle ceiling is too low for me to stand up in. There are times when I like this approach, when there really is nothing to say or do or any reason to be considerate. Sucking is all that matters. The guy is hungry and good at what he does and I don't have to worry too much about making him gag.

Another theory: Most men have an oral capacity to match their dick size.

His hair is tied up in two small buns, one at the nape, the other closer to the top of his head. I take out the rubber bands and dig my fingers into his hair – it is dense and heavy and reaches down to his shoulders. I have always loved long hair. When I was in my twenties I had hair halfway down my back, thick curly light-brown hair, streaks of it bleached by the sun. Now my hair is cropped close to my skull. In some strange way, grasping his hair in my fists makes me think of that time. I was probably about the same age he is now, and my waist – 28" back then – was as slim as his is. I was never as skinny as him, or rather, I never felt myself to be, and my cock was never as big as his; his must be a good 2" bigger than mine.

"Do you want to come?" I say.

"Just hold me," he says.

"How?" I say.

"Lie down," he says. "On your side, facing me."

"Like this?" I say.

"Yes," he says. "Now put your arms around me."

His name is David; he' a flight attendant with Air Namibia. He tells me that earlier he'd been upstairs with a guy who'd fucked him. He's usually the one on top, he says, but the guy was really nice.

"So I let him," he says.

"What about me?" I say.

"You're nice," he says.

"Is that my cue?" I say.

But the cubicles at the sauna in Waterloo are too small for anything more than the missionary position. What with the low sloping ceilings, doggy style in particular can be a bit cramped. The doors to the cubicles are these three-quarter steel things. The brick-work is exposed. The mattresses are black. It's all a bit – *gay*. Very New-York-loft-apartment. Some cubicles don't have light bulbs, so all you get is the faint light coming in from the gap between the top of the door and its frame. David and I stroke each other and continue to kiss while we go through the where-you-from, how-long-you-been-here, do-you-miss-the-sun – *I do!* – questions, until someone opens the door and pokes his head in and sees us lying there, our arms around each other, whispering.

13. Natural Disasters Pair Activity

"The good thing about teaching Weather," McKenzie says. "It's always in the news."

"Literally," I say.

She tells me she did a session on natural disasters, divided the class into pairs and gave them words like catastrophe, emergency, tragedy, casualty to explain to each other. Then she gave them a topic: Tourism in the time of tsunamis?

"But at some point," she says. "It became clear that everyone knew someone who'd died or got lost in an earthquake.

"And here we are," I say. "Getting all upset about the fucking ash cloud over Europe."

"All it means is that the homos get to extend their holidays wherever they are," she says. "Europe," she says. "I mean, what the fuck."

She's right. Mario the Italian is in town and he can't get back to Rome. Eyjafjallajökull is erupting, so him and I had gone to Fortnum's for tea the day before yesterday. Peppermint tea and a chocolate slice for him, apple pie and a Royal Blend for me. And he sat there telling me about this sex club he'd gone to the night before.

"But I didn't do nothing," he says.

"What kind of club?" I say.

"Everyone was naked," he says.

"No underpants?"

"Just the boots," he says.

"These ones?" I say, reaching under the table to touch his black leather boot.

I undo the zip on the side of his boot and stroke his leg while he tells me about this American guy he chatted to once online who squatted over a plastic sheet in his living room and shat on the floor. All this via webcam, so that Mario could be an audience to the Texan as he rubbed excrement onto his own face and chest.

"This is too much," Mario says. "I turn off at that minute."

"There must be something about it you liked," I say.

"I want to be insulted," he says. (Pronouncing it in-sool-ted.)

"Like what?" I say. "Like: You fucking faggot?"

He smiles.

"Do you like being on all fours?" I say.

"I do," he says.

"Like a dog?" I say.

"Yes," he says. "I would be somebody's dog."

"And you'll do whatever I tell you?" I say.

"Yes," he says, his body trembling as if he's been waiting a long time for this moment, so thrilled he can't contain himself.

"You're my dog," I say.

"Yes," he says. "I want to be your dog."

I pay the bill and lead him to the Fortnum and Mason toilets, to a cubicle surprisingly small for a department store where the Queen apparently does an occasional shop. The guy doesn't want to kiss. His lips are open just a fraction and we talk into each other's mouths.

"I want to be your slave," he says.

"Turn around," I say. "Show me your arse."

And he does. Immediately. He turns his head to look at me, just a flicker of doubt in his eyes, so tiny, before he spreads his cheeks to show off his hole, a lovely soft, clean and odourless bud.

"You are making me *orni*," he says.

"Oh, shut up with that stupid fucking Italian accent," I say.

"Sorry," he says. "When I get it wrong, I want you to punish me."

His cock is right above my rucksack and he's oblivious, jerking himself off frantically. I don't want him coming all over my bag. I don't want him coming at all. I'm worried that when he comes that'll be it, the magic broken, my desire left hanging in mid-air. But he comes.

"Okay, now go," I say.

"What?" he says.

"You're disgusting," I say.

"No, you did not say that," McKenzie says. "You did not."

"I sure did," I say, "and he'd looked at me all hurt and surprised."

"Poor guy," she says.

"Turns out we all have our limitations," I say. "Even the masochists among us need a tender goodbye.

14. Expanding the Repertoire

On Thursday night – later than I usually go out for sex – at about 10pm, I head for naked night at the sex club. If Mario can do it, so can I! The night's called Stripped, as opposed to the Night of Underwear. A few months ago – I hadn't mentioned this to Mario, so as not to give him the impression we had something in common – I'd gone to the sex club's underwear night by mistake, thinking it was just the regular fully-clothed night, and the guy at the desk had said, go on, you'll like it. And I did.

When I left, he told me they had a naked night, and that I should come back for that.

"One step at a time," I'd said.

Three months later, maybe more, emboldened and intrigued by Mario's stories, I'm here. The dress-code is strict – footwear is all you're allowed.

I'm not sure why I'd hesitated, what it was about the naked night that had turned me off, scared me, because I love the feeling of walking into a crowded sex club, entering a room full of men all there for the same reason. It reminds me of the first gay bar I walked into, a place called the Theatre Club. I was about twenty-one, and a guy I'd met at an anti-war demonstration had taken me there.

Tonight the sex club is heaving. Everyone, except the bar staff and the clothes-check guy, is naked. Men walk around holding onto their cocks, fluffing them; this is not the place to come with a small willy – you're constantly being scanned for your size. Some men have very large penises and on a night like this these men are popular. I watch a nice big chunky guy with a nice big chunky cock fuck a tall slim guy over a barrel (the barrels are there to rest your drinks on), but he fucks like a masturbator, like a ham-actor in a porn movie. He holds onto the guy's arse and shoulder so that he can pull himself deeper into his arse, and he just bangs away, his hands locked in the same position.

I'm thinking: *At least stroke the guy.*

When it comes to penises, I'm more of a grower than a shower. Limp, my cock is not impressive, and it just wouldn't get hard. At some point I thought, fuck it, I'm going to stand here with a small cock and I don't care what people think. It'll be my act of defiance. A couple of guys try to get it hard, but the whole atmosphere isn't turning me on; the small crowd that has gathered to watch the fucking, and the two guys themselves, seem bored, anaesthetized by the metronomic thrusting. I keep thinking about Freud's observation about concealment: men in underwear are so much sexier.

Just as I am getting ready to leave, albeit reluctantly, because I like being here, the heat, the proximity of other bodies, the rawness of it all, and the surprise moments of tenderness and connection, like when the short brown guy comes up to me and starts playing with my nipples. "Nice," he says. And it is nice, and his tits are nice, those lovely long nipples you find on some black men. I play with them while he plays with mine. At some point he plays with my cock, which is hard by then, and I play with his, which is soft.

"Have you been here a long time?" I say.

"It's the poppers," he says. "And yes, a good few hours."

"Where you from?" I say.

"Florida," he says.

But his accent is something else, somewhere in the Caribbean, maybe Martinique. I hold him close to me and he turns around, puts his shoulders to my chest; he's much shorter than me. I keep playing with his nipples, rubbing my hands over his velvet-smooth chest. Every now and then he tilts his head back and reaches for my mouth and we kiss and I put my open palm on his throat and push down on it.

"Nice," he says.

"You like that?" I say.

"Uh-huh," he says.

He has a word tattooed across the top of his back, arching from shoulder-blade to shoulder-blade, the same kind of font David Beckham has used to ink BROOKLYN onto his lower back, just above his arse. I don't remember what the word was on the Florida guy's back, and maybe I never knew; he was too close for me to read without my glasses on.

It's almost one, close to closing time, when I leave the club and cycle towards home, along Euston Road, late-night traffic to my right, past the Wellcome Institute, large posters advertising its Identity Exhibition, Eight Rooms, Nine Lives, then St Pancras Station where I sometimes like to go and sit and have an espresso at Paul, the cafe, just to feel like I'm about to travel somewhere, like I could hop on a train to Paris. At home, I run a bath and listen to the silence coming from outside, that stillness, with everyone in the neighbourhood asleep and the cars on Blackstock Road inaudible.

15. The Masseur

After a while, if I don't get touched deeply, or hugged, or sleep with someone all night and wake with them in the morning, my sense of self becomes diffuse, my boundaries – murky; my body craves some form of containment. Often, a massage is the answer, so, on Sunday, after a weekend of working near Marble Arch, I visited the sauna nearby, a sauna that caters mainly for older men and their admirers.

The sauna is in the basement of a big building, down a flight of stairs that looks like it should lead to a bin room, or a bomb shelter. I like that underworld feel; it's the same kind of entrance to the sex club off Tottenham Court Road.

The guy at the desk is always friendly. The place is clean and small. Most of the saunas I've been to in London never seem to get the heat right – either they're too hot or not hot enough, so you land up sitting on a bench that's too cold for a steam room. This place is perfect. While I wait for my massage, I make out with a Chinese guy who's a great kisser, who plays with my nipples and likes to be slapped. His breath smells a bit funny, though, like there's something off about it, like he's eaten... I don't know... an omelette, perhaps, or maybe he just hasn't brushed his teeth.

The surprise is the next guy, an Asian guy much hairier than I usually go for, but there aren't many men to choose from and we're alone in the dry sauna, both on the same wooden bench and I ask if he's having fun and we get chatting and one thing leads to another and he compliments me on my chest and kneads my shoulders and offers to give me a massage, so we land up in a room.

He has strong hands and knows how to massage. I can tell he likes my body, likes digging his fingers into my flesh, and while he concentrates on my back, I stroke his leg, up and down, gently, until I want to surrender myself completely and I take his cock down my throat. And what a great cock it is. Lots more happened. We had good sex and talked a bit and said we'd do it again. He said he comes to the sauna every Sunday and that I should come back to see him.

"How long's your massage for?" he says.

"An hour," I say. "Will you still be here?"

"I'll wait for you," he says.

And he does.

The official massage was exactly what I wanted: deep, with lots of hand-work, as opposed to elbow-work. That hour on the massage table was a time to pause... to breathe.. London is so often the opposite of calm, and we learn to live in its commotion, thrive on the flurry, especially those of us with what Virginia Woolf called a "squirrel cage mind". What else would I write about, I think, if I couldn't dart in and out of these places to refresh my stagnancy.

The massage guy offered me "extras" towards the end, without an undertone of sleaze, just a friendly, but businesslike "would you like any extras?" He was gracious about it. I wished I could say yes, that I *wanted* to say yes, but it takes me a while to come and a hand-job would have taken ages.

Besides, Hanif was waiting for me.

Hanif tells me he's into Bears. I tell him I hate being called a Bear, because when someone says "Bear" all I hear is FAT!

And now that I'm home and writing this and Hanif's already friended me on Facebook, I see that a lot of his friends *are* Bears, as in: FAT. *Is that what I look like?* I think. Maybe it makes things easier if you have a type, if you can acknowledge what kind of guys you're into and then just go for them. Yes, I'm into tall, slim smooth guys. What would it be like if I said to myself that I'm into that kind of guy and that's who I want to have sex with. It would give me focus, but wouldn't it be limiting? It's always satisfying to find a guy who's your type, and it's disorienting to discover you're someone else's and that they're with you because of that. Hanif fancied me because I ticked his boxes.

16. Be Nice

I'm about seventeen I'm at a friend's house and we're about to sit down for dinner when his father says something about what lovely long fingers I have, an artist's hands, he calls them. And that lingers. Good things linger. Someone says nice things about my body, how handsome I'm looking, and it's like the first time I'm hearing nice words. I don't remember many nice things being said to me. Until I started fucking around.

Quite a few men have said nice things in the saunas and sex clubs and cruising grounds around the world. And because of that, because I got to a point where I had to believe them, I started taking in the nice things people said to me, about my clothes, about my thoughts, my gestures. Nice things linger, and accumulate.

Like earlier this afternoon I was sitting on a deck chair cooling off by the pool at the sauna when a man comes up to me, a guy in his late twenties, soft and smooth, a thin gold chain around his neck.

"I just wanted to tell you that you're beautiful," he says.

"Oh," I say. "Thank you."

"I love all this flesh," he says. "All this size."

"Thank you."

"I'm not your type, am I?" he says.

I smile at him, apologetic. Still, he sits down on the arm of the sun-lounger.

"Where are you from?" he says.

"London," I say.

"No, but before that," he says.

"Let's just say London," I say.

"Well, you're the hairiest Londoner I've ever met," he says, and touches my chest, rubs his palm over it. Then he gets up and moves away down the corridor, disappearing into the steam room or the jacuzzi or into the labyrinth of rooms upstairs.

I notice that I'm smiling to myself, that I want to laugh out loud. Such attention is always a surprise to me, a reminder of something that should have been. I'm feeling horny and sexy and I must be giving off that vibe, because people are responding.

One guy in the dry sauna positions himself on the bench below me so that I can slide my cock into his mouth. He takes my hand and puts it at the back of his head and makes it clear he wants me to force his mouth onto my cock. He wants to gag. I put my hand in his mouth and feel the back of his throat. I love feeling the back of a guy's throat with the tips of my fingers, getting as much of my fist inside him so that his mouth feels like an arse.

"I'm good, yes?" he says.

"You're good," I say.

"I'm a bitch," he says.

"Uh-huh," I say.

"A cock-sucking bitch," he says, which is not really turning me on, not because I don't like those words,

47

but it's starting to feel like the guy's taking it too seriously, like he really wants to be humiliated, bullied. I don't mind when it's a game, a fantasy, but sometimes you come across a guy who really wants that, who has such a deep longing for others to hate him – *just use and abuse me, then kick me out* – that it feels like you're coming face to face with a demon, someone's "alter" and I want to run a mile. So I get up and head for the showers.

Later, in another part of the sauna, in the dark group-sex room with its raised platform that fits about ten guys with standing room around it, like some small black-box theatre, this other guy gets down on his knees in the dark and swallows my cock. He does that thing I love almost more than anything else: he raises his hands and starts playing with the tips of my nipples.

His hair's in a pony tail. I'm thinking perhaps he's Columbian, or Thai – his skin has that kind of softness and he seems brown; his hair – black and smooth. Only when we get up, when we leave the dark room and head for a more well-lighted place and he lets his hair down, do I see how long it is – almost halfway down his back – thick and lush.

Every hole of his is open and welcoming. It's that kind of sex. We've moved to a cubicle and are having great sex. He's from Thailand, from Bangkok…

"Not a good place to be now," I say.

"No," he agrees. "Not good."

"Are your family okay?" I say.

"My family fine," he says. "They live outside Bangkok, in suburb."

He's been here for ten years, has had an English boyfriend since he got here, a school teacher, and still his English is elementary.

"Do you still have sex with your boyfriend?" I say.

"Oh, no," he says. "No sex."

"But you sleep together," I say.

"Yes, yes," he says. "In same bed."

But this conversation probably happened after we had sex, after I fucked him, his arsehole soft and relaxed (my favourite) and he'd made appreciative noises and I'd felt like I could keep going for hours, but I got tired and I lay down for a bit and he went back to my cock. Long story short: I came.

I'm quite loud when I come. Most men like it, or don't care one way or another. Some guys get freaked out by the noise. I dated a guy once who got so embarrassed, he told me to keep it down, that he didn't want the neighbours to hear. I like being loud. The lesbian couple two floors down from my flat are loud, and it's a kind of call to them, a thread of queer camaraderie that stretches between the third and first floors. But what happens next at the sauna has lingered.

From the cubicle adjacent to ours a barrage of lube sachets comes raining down from over the dividing wall. About ten sachets, and then again, and both times I throw two back, playfully, as in WTF. But it leaves a bitter taste in my mouth. It seems odd and unfriendly. A very English thing to do; to not say anything, but rather to act aggressively, not even passive aggressively. I thought it might be someone I knew, someone who recognised my voice, like the guy who was embarrassed by my orgasm noises, a guy I'd met in this very sauna, and with whom I'd had sex in one of these cubicles. But it wasn't.

"They could have said something nice," I said to the Thai guy. "They could have laughed."

Conspiratorially, I thought.

Aren't we all in this together?

My cell-mate said it was jealousy. He said: "Some people see you have fun and they jealous." Which seemed like it might be true, but I've never been comfortable with the concept of people being jealous, of wanting something I had, of being envious.

Bad things have a whole history of bad things to latch onto, and they threaten to linger for longer. Every queer boy who's been bullied will tell you this. Bad things take up space. Their shelf-life is indefinite. But the good lingered, too. The intimacy with the Thai guy. Massaging each other, kissing, talking casually and lying together for another ten or twenty minutes, then getting hard again. Afterwards, we'd gone downstairs for a shower, only to discover, standing there under the water, that I'd left the condom on.

"Tacky," I said, and we'd laughed, conspiratorially.

I got dressed and headed home on my bike, stopping off at Tesco's on Shoreditch High Street for milk and apples, and some fresh chocolate croissants which I ate this morning on the balcony in the sun.

17. Talking About Experiences

"What if you fall in love with one of these guys?" McKenzie says.

We're in the noodle bar, in a booth, where we like to be. It's cosy, our own private something in the restaurant.

And sometimes, because I've been hanging out with her for a while now, because she's such a daddy and the occasional person calls her sir, I forget that my friend's a lesbian. Until a question like this comes along. A question about love!

"Unlikely," I say.

Because a long time ago I'd stopped seeing these encounters as potential beginnings. They are what they are, framed by time; on average: a therapeutic hour. And I've adapted my expectations accordingly. Only rarely (read: almost never) do I arrange to meet outside the space.

"I used to fall in love every time," I say. "But you get used to beautiful men."

"How long have you been doing this?" she says.

"What?" I say. "Whoring around?"

She nods, and the waiter arrives with our plates of yaki soba – steaming brown noodles with bits of chicken and little shrimps, flecks of spring onion, and as a garnish on top: strips of pickled pink ginger – so we sit back as she puts them on the table, then raise our chopsticks and get stuck in.

"I've been a slut since I was seventeen," I say, comforted by the salty soft noodles.

"I could have used that in class," she says.

They'd been doing the Past Perfect Continuous, mixed in with discussions about marital status. I *have been* single *for...* You *have been* married *since...* She *has been* dating that guy *since... for...*

And in a Japanese accent, I say: "I hava beena a slutta for terty yeah," I say.

"Good," she says. "Well done, Mykashi."

"And what examples did *you* give?" I say. "I have been single since... Class, I have been a daddy for..."

"Oh, yeah, sure," she says. "Class, I have been worshipping high femmes since high school."

"Well done, McKenzie," I say. "Do you want to tell us more?"

I pick at the bits of chicken and shrimp with my chopsticks. The noodles I raise in threads and shovel into my mouth, like gathering wool, while I listen to McKenzie talk about the woman she's been chatting to on Skype, this gallery owner from New York who wants to see McKenzie's work when she comes over to London at the end of the summer.

"She's kinky," McKenzie says.

"Yeah," I say. "But is she kinky enough?"

18. Soft Men

Often, after dinner with McKenzie, I go to the Liverpool Street sauna. The noodle bar is not far from there, and it's on my cycle route home. Dinner had been good and I felt good and yes, even though I don't like to admit it, I guess I have to agree with McKenzie that despite all the things I moan about – money, my mother, more time to myself – life is good. I felt that when I parked my bike outside the sauna. I felt sexy. I felt in my body and good about my body and on days like this... ah, yes, on days like this... God shines his light I get the gifts I've been wishing for.

Hector is 28 and Brazilian, a man with vigour, with elasticity to his skin; he is not a man winding down into domesticity and loss. He has left a country and a boyfriend and a job, and come to London to start from scratch. He has come to Europe to make it. I tell him I came to London at about the same age, but without the money or the job prospects.

He said I ticked every box.

If I have to talk about boxes, I'd say Hector ticked enough of mine to make for intense sex. The main box he ticked was that he liked sex. He liked me licking inside his nostrils and he had nice nostrils to lick. The best nostrils are either smooth or unclipped; brittle hairs are not always pleasing to the tongue. Hector had lovely soft hairs in his and I licked and licked and let my tongue linger inside, one nostril at a time, the right in particular, and then we kissed.

"*And* he's a good kisser," he said, looking at me and smiling and making the gesture of ticking a box.

Sometimes I have sex with someone and I feel their whole body is there, everything is there, and I'm there, too (mostly there, more or less, because, really, I'm such a control freak I hardly ever let go – as in: never)... but no, I *was* there and I breathed into his mouth, passing the air back and forth, and I lifted him up and played with his arsehole and he sucked my cock and I sucked his, which was considerably bigger, but still I took it all the way to the base, all the way to the back of my throat and I could tell he was happy. This swallowing of his cock was making him happy and I wanted him to slap my face... I didn't say this to him at first, but I said it to him a while later after we'd both come and were lying together on the mattress and he'd slapped my bum lightly and I'd said he's welcome to slap my face anytime but not to slap my bum.

"Do you like that?" he says.

"The slapping in the face?"

"Si," he says.

"Anything but the bum," I say. "It's too much like punishment."

I remember... well, actually, I don't remember, but my brother tells me that when we were younger my father took me into his bedroom and whacked me with his belt. Again and again and again. My brother says he thinks I was being punished for something *he* did. And later, I remember that I'd forgotten my Afrikaans text book at home and Mr Lategaan made me bend over the front desk, to face the rest of the class so that he could thump me with his T-rule over and over again. And another memory, earlier: My hair was not short enough for Mr Feinstein, so I was taken to the principal's office and in front of Mr Povey I was caned again and again – two of the best – and then made to say: Thank-you, sir.

"But the face is okay?" Hector says.

"I think so," I say. I've never tried it, but I like the idea."

19. Playing with Our Dogs

What kind of dog you got, mate? He's a rottie, mate. You want to bring him over? Bring him over. I want to suck on that dog cock, mate. Fuck yeah, he's got a great cock. I fucking love sucking on dog cock. And you, mate, what kind of dog you got? She's a rottie as well, mate, a rottie bitch, mate, fucking beautiful pussy, dark on the outside but when you open it up it's all pink inside, mate. You want to see her pussy, you want to fucking lick that pussy, mate? Yeah, mate, you and me get down and fucking lick her dog pussy together. Fuck, yeah, taste that pussy, mate. Fucking beautiful. Fucking smelly pussy. She fucking loves it. You can open her legs, mate, just pull them open wider, get your tongue in there, really fucking lick her cunt, beautiful fucking dog pussy. Taste good, mate? You want to bring your rottie over, mate? Bring him over so I can taste his fucking dog cock. You like dog cock, mate? Stinking fucking dog cock. Lick his arse, as well, mate. It's dirty, mate, fucking dirty. I fucking love that, fucking love that shitty arsehole, that dog's shitter, get my tongue right in there, mate. You don't mind, mate, do you? You don't mind if I fucking lick your dog's shithole. Nah, mate, you fucking do it – he fucking loves it. I'll fucking kiss the dog, man, fucking get my tongue into his mouth, really fucking taste that dog breath. Fuck, yeah, mate. I'll get the rottie bitch to lick out your fucking hole. Fucking right, mate. You just keep fingering her pussy, get her pussy ready for your cock, mate. You ready to put your cock into her pussy? Really fucking slide it in, mate. Fuck, yeah, fucking beautiful. Beautiful tight pussy. Yeah, mate, keep your big fucking cock inside her, let her get used to it, let her really fucking get used to that massive cock, mate.

And so it goes.

I've spoken to him before. His profile message says he's "into canine" and he has this crazed kind of voice that I love, a voice that reflects a mind willing to go the extra mile. I don't imagine his life, not what his room looks like or what he does for a living or even what *he* looks like. It's just him and his voice and the demented extremes of his imagination. It's not the subject matter. It's more about the hunger, the urgency, the thrill, as if this is something essential, so real, so captivating, so all-consuming that it's as good as sex, and as necessary.

When I say *his* voice, I mean my voice, too.

20. Words

An email attachment arrives from my mother with a PowerPoint presentation by a Peruvian philosopher about his alleged conversation with the Dalai Lama. I'm convinced it's fake. But words are words, no matter who said them first, and sometimes they stick, they hit a mark, they disrupt. I like that. I like words that ruffle my feathers, that shake me up. But then there are words that make me feel ashamed, or guilty, and maybe that's a good thing, maybe I should be pausing to think about some of the stuff I'm doing, or not doing (like letting wars happen, and poverty, and unnecessary death).

What this PowerPoint thing said was: "Watch your thoughts, for they become words. Watch your words, for they become actions. Watch your actions, for they become habits. Watch your habits, for they become character. Watch your character, for it becomes your destiny." Ralph Waldo Emerson said, before all this, that thoughts become words, and words become deeds, and deeds become habits, and habits – character. And character is everything.

He'd been reading the Upanishads.

The source doesn't matter. The truth belongs to everyone. I thought about all the phone sex I've been having and how so much of it is about fucking women and being brutal, but sometimes not – there's one guy I speak to who worships the yoni. Him and I get off saying "pussy pussy pussy" to each other, whispering in each other's ear: gash, slit, wet pussy, penis for pussy, cock made for pussy, worship pussy, I love pussy, pussy, pussy, open pussy, take me in, pussy, swallow me, eat me, I need pussy, I kneel before pussy, before the slit, the gash, the godlike cunt of woman... That sort of thing. But most of the time it's hard and brutal and as fucked up as Tom Cruise in *Magnolia*:

"Respect the cock. Tame the cunt."

But I tell myself it's fantasy and it's in my head and I would never do that to anyone, never be so violent or humiliate anyone. Yet, having said all that, I'm finding that phone-sex *is* effecting the way I am with people. Sometimes I feel strange when I'm with women, usually in those quiet moments when we're not speaking and I think about how the night before I'd jerked off with some guy on the phone and we'd talked about taking it in turns to fuck some bird, how he'd hold her legs back so I could get a good look at her cunt and he'd watch me slide my cock in, really shove it into her beautiful shaved cunt, all pink and wet, flaps opening up and her clit swollen and me flicking it and pinching it while he did the same with her tits and rammed his cock down her throat. Make her choke, man. Make the bitch gag on that monster cock. And then the next day, I'm here with McKenzie talking about the Tories ruining the education system, and we're sitting close to each other, and we'll hug each other, or put a hand on each other, stroke each other because we appreciate each other's company, and we've known each other for a long time, from before I started having sex on the phone with strangers... these actions that have become a habit, and this habit that has become part of my character. And there is a part of me that fears I will one day go too far, that I will do something inappropriate, that I will be walking around the classroom and I will touch someone, I will lean towards a student who has come to the staff room to ask me a question and I will kiss her on the mouth.

21. The Glorious Days of Underwear

So I'm trying to cut down. If I had to say how many times I've come in the last two weeks and not been happy about it, or happy about what led up to the ejaculating, I'd have to say at least twice, and those times involved phone sex. Yesterday, when I needed a break from working and wanted to go to the sex club because Sunday is the day of underwear, I thought maybe I should stay home and not rush out to have sex with strangers every time a window opens up in my schedule.

I set out with a degree of ambivalence, but I came home elated, transformed by the power of men together in an underground bar, all naked and enjoying each other. True pleasure happens in silence, in the unspoken. (True terror, too, but that's another story.) I felt I was back in my body and my body was a thing of joy, appreciated.

To tell of one gesture one must tell everything.

His name is Luis. It must have been about 3pm and I'd only just arrived. There's something special about Underwear-Only Sundays, the afternoon gathering of men in a black-walled subterranean bar not far from Tottenham Court Road. Something leisurely.

Luis was in boxer shorts.

He was Spanish, young and dark and muscled, shorter than me, a sprinkling of hair on his chest, a substantial cock... and he played well with my tits, touched me and... (I'd only been there five minutes!) brought me back to life, out of the murky waters of the subconscious. He was everything I wanted at that moment, and I didn't stop myself from showing it; I moaned loudly, growled, a kind of amplified purr while he sucked on my tits and my cock, his lips soft and engulfing. We kissed with gusto, me and him slobbering at each other, without vulgarity or inhibition, like we could consume each other, drinking like animals at a trough.

And so it went for about twenty minutes until I felt I was going to come. But I wanted more men, I wanted to be touched more, by others, to kiss, to have my cock sucked, to be appreciated and stroked and admired. My hunger was growing.

All this is just to set the scene for that one gesture that came in the middle of our afternoon.

Luis and I parted ways for a while and said we'd see each other later.

In the interim: Two English guys. One with a very hairy chest and long nipples. We made out in the main public area – there by the barrels. He had this strange smell, though, a mixture of poppers and alcohol, maybe his lunch, too, a cheese and pickle sandwich, a combination that was slightly off-putting, but pleasing enough to keep at it for a while, though not enough for any longer than that.

"I was just taking a break," I said.

"Oh, sorry," he said. "I'll leave you to it."

The other English guy was smooth and lean and defined. "Defined": that strange euphemism used only by men who are not. Guys who *are* defined usually refer to themselves as athletic or muscular.

The smooth English guy was athletic and muscular.

It's kind of a long story how we landed up sitting on a sofa together and him going down on his knees before me to suck on my cock, but it went a little something like this:

"I do like sucking cock," he said, as we set there in our underwear on the sofa, chatting, our shoulders touching, talking about what we liked as if deciding what to order from a menu. "And I like getting fucked," he said.

"Do you like having a hand on the back of your head and getting a cock shoved to the back of your throat?" I said, my leg against his.

My God, his skin was beautiful.

"Uh-huh," he said.

"Do you like a cock banging into you so that you choke?" I said.

"I do," he said.

"I think that's your cue," I said.

It was nice, him on his knees with my cock in his mouth. Yes, faint praise, but there's something about the English and the shape of their hunger. It's an odd kind of hunger, even when it's full-on, and I like a full-on hunger... it's just... I don't know... odd. Prissy. Even the guys I've met who are into fisting and bondage and leather and other hardcore stuff, they're still prissy. They lay out their arm-sized dildos neatly on fluffy white towels. They keep their tit-clamps and vibrators in neat little drawers by their bedside. They do everything, but they won't, for example, kiss you after you've rimmed them. And they love being rimmed.

I have known a few English men who are not prissy at all. But they seem to be the exception.

The smooth English guy was not into nipples.

"I'm not as bad as I used to be," he says "A year ago I wouldn't let anyone touch them."

"That would be a deal breaker for me," I say.

Soon afterwards, Luis and I meet up again. There is something endearing about a man who keeps his word, who does what he 'd said he'd do. I expect men to keep their word, though I am aware of the context I'm operating in. And there we were, in that corner of the club where those small cubicles are, the ones just big enough for two to stand in, Luis and I facing each other, a metre or so between us.

Other men were kissing him, and I watched them play with his cock and go down to suck it. I watched them touch him. But it was as if we were alone in that room together, in that space in the corner, as if, when we looked at each other, everyone else fell away. It was all that, that kind of cliché, but it was something sexier, too. It was as if those men were necessary to our connection, part of it. I loved watching them enjoying his body, and I knew that only an hour ago he'd been doing the same to me, that he'd been on his haunches with my cock in his mouth.

Luis had his men and I had mine: a tall slim guy to my right, a short buff guy to my left. I touched the slim guy, stroked his back, drew him closer to me so he could put a nipple in his mouth. The other guy came closer, short enough to suck on the other nipple without bending down, and I held onto both of them, pressed their heads to my chest. And all the while I kept my eyes on Luis, as if to mesmerise him, to let him know he was the one, that he, above all others, was the most desirable and most beautiful.

I drew nearer.

I reached out my hand and stroked his shoulder, round and smooth, his neck, his face, freshly shaved, the contours of his cheeks, his nose, his eyelids, his forehead, gently, and he in turn lifted his hand out of the scrum of men and stroked my arm, touched my nipple. I moved closer – slowly – as if moving through history, through time, through a million abstract things that keep men apart – ignorance, bigotry, shame, fear – just to be with Luis.

The gesture was in the way we touched each other over the heads of other men. We were surrounded by others, and I chose him and he chose me. That was the moment. That's all. I reached out and touched him and he did the same, and we stood there, suspended, frozen, melting, as still as if we were in a Bill Viola video piece. Only the patient would notice what was happening. Only those who stood still long enough would see the full arc of our gesture.

Time passes. A day. A week.

Luis will be here in about an hour's time. He will arrive on his bike. He has been to the gym. From what I've seen, he looks perfect in a loose grey vest, the vest he wore when we cycled home from the sex club, our flats just a short distance apart. In my fantasy we will have sex when he gets here, we will lie in bed and talk, then go for a bike ride to a place with trees and grass, perhaps the Heath, where we'll sit and talk and drink pomegranate juice, then we'll wonder deeper into the woods where men go in search of other men, and there – Luis and I, connected amongst them, on a day like today, the 3rd of July, as the homosexuals party in Soho – we will fuck.

22. Those Meant-to-Be Days

By the end of the month the Indus has overflowed and Pakistan is flooded. Seven million acres of land are underwater. Roads and bridges are swept away; fourteen million people are displaced; two thousand are dead. In Punjab, rice crops, cotton, sugarcane and mango groves are lost. Haiti in January, this in July, now we just have to wait and see what December will bring.

"What the fuck," McKenzie says. "Is God some fucking white guy or what? Kill the blecks. Kill the Muslims. Who's next?"

"There were the Chinese in April," I say.

"You know what I'm saying," she says.

We're on the terrace at the Hampstead Theatre drinking white wine. It's a mild evening and we've just seen a play called *The House of Bilquis Bibi* (not very good). Our friend, Zaid, a kathak dancer who also teaches at the College, was leading a Q&A after the show and got us free tickets. One of the questions to the panel of artists and directors had been about a utopian world: What would the ideal world to create in look like, geographically and linguistically. Would it be a world with multiples of you, a place with sunshine and sea and people who understand the languages you spoke? Is that a utopian world? And what would you need in order to feel inspired? A world that you know nothing of, in which everything is unfamiliar, and yet to be welcomed in it, to be made to feel safe, unthreatened by what is new and unknown?

"Human being can't help seeing outsiders as invaders," one of the panellists had said. "If you feel threatened you're not going to be welcoming. What the English need to ask themselves is will they ever get over feeling threatened. Because really, it's all projection. They're the ones whose wealth and identity are built on invading and ransacking other places... why *wouldn't* they assume people want to do the same to them?"

"Then how do we, as artists, operate under those conditions?" Zaid said.

"Leave," McKenzie whispers, loud enough for a couple of people sitting next to us to chuckle.

The terrace looks out onto an open courtyard. It's after ten at night and the sky is clear, almost indigo, with a glowing azure colour at the far edges, as if this were a sky untouched by clouds, the way a new cloth shines, pristine and smooth and open, like a canvas, like an empty stage. The three of us sit there, me and McKenzie, and Zaid in his golden silk kurta. A sudden silence has appeared, a gentle lull, most of the patrons gone, until Zaid laughs and remembers: "I heard your little intervention, babes," he says to McKenzie.

"Good," she says. "It was meant to be a stage whisper."

"Maybe that suspicion on their part," I say, "the English, their not totally embracing us, Asians, Jews, people of colour, queers is what an artist needs. We don't even have to work to be outsiders."

"Then we're never really resisting," McKenzie says. "What we make is never really in conversation with the world around us. If you're ignoring the master, you'll never topple him."

"Art *must* resistant," Zaid says. "*And*, babes, the trick is to ignore them in order go inwards, to find the core of what we want to say, and still resist."

And so the conversation goes, and while we talk I think about the best way to cycle from Swiss Cottage to... what's the closest sauna? Or should I go through Regent's Park and towards Warren Street to catch the last couple of hours at the sex club? It's a relief not have to prepare classes, not to think about what needs to be photocopied... it's summer and time feels like a flowing stream; all I need to do is hop into my kayak and glide.

His touch is more than his kiss. His touch and the way he holds me and presses up close, the way he lets me hold him, cling to him, both of us – yes, two boys clinging – our bodies warming each other. It's one of those meant-to-be days.

He's a bit shorter than me, a hairy chest, a short beard, hairy arms and legs and arse. Nice and firm, and a cock that reveals itself to be substantial.

I like a substantial cock and I enjoy sucking it when we go for a swim and he sits on the edge of the pool and I stand in the water facing his crotch, for all to see! and suck hungrily on his fat, long, just-the-right-size cock, all the way to the base to feel the gag that satisfies.

Later, in a cubicle upstairs, we realise we know each other from some years back. We'd connected here one evening and spent a few hours fooling around and talking, the kind of intense conversation that sometimes happens in the sauna.

This time we land up talking about death and about mindfulness and Jon Kabat Zinn, whom Liam has been studying.

"I like listening to his CDs in the bath," I say.

We talk about our fathers who are dead, about the way they died, those days of silence before their spirits left their bodies. Liam says he dreams about his father, who died only a year ago, late, in his seventies. He says: In the dream my father takes me to see God, and he says, Liam, what do you want to say to God?

"I howled at God," Liam says.

In another dream his father watched him jump from one stepping-stone to the next, seven of them, and then plunge into the water.

"It was a good dream," he says.

All this while we're having sex, while my cock is inside him and we're kissing, his lips strong and thick, like the lips of some black men I've known. I say: I could eat your mouth. That's what I say. I say: I want your mouth in my mouth; I want to bite your lips off and feel them on my tongue, taste your blood in my mouth.

"Does that scare you?" I say.

He says: "What?"

I say: "That I want your blood in my mouth."

"Scared?" he says, slapping his cock against my stomach, his big thick hard cock. "Does this look like I'm scared?" he says: "What other part of my body would you want?"

I want to say *I love you*. To say this while we are fucking and I'm telling him to talk to me in Gaelic while I talk to him in Afrikaans, even though it's not that great, while I tell him that he is mine, that his hole is mine, that I want to be inside him, that he is my baby, and I want to be able to say I love you, to feel, as I sometimes do, that I have fallen in love with a man I barely know.

He says his father died of cancer. He says he died in his bed at 3.27 in the morning.

"I listened to his last breath," Liam says.

I say I was with my dad, too, but I don't remember the time of his death. Ten years have passed since then. Ten years of just-yesterdays.

We are two men naked in a box. He says to use saliva, that saliva is best, that he's always preferred saliva, not lube. He doesn't want those chemicals inside him. I say I wish I could make a film of this, to be in this cubicle, this box with its pale yellow walls, its black ceiling, to make a film of us in here for three days. I say there are days I come to the sauna and I know what I want and I wish for what I want and I get it.

"Today is one of those days," I say.

He says nothing. I ask him if he understands what I've just said, and he says yes, yes, I understand.

We are two men naked in a box, lying like snakes. He says for a long time he told his lover he was born in the Year of the Horse, when really, he was a Snake. He is, it is clear to see, in this limited world of penises, both snake and horse. He says this one small lie, the lie he told his lover, who is no longer his lover — *eleven years?* I said, because I remembered him telling me this last time — a man much younger than him — that one lie complicated everything, led to more lies.

"But that's a long time ago," he says.

We lie in silence. We lie there quietly, me and him, a man I hardly know, but with whom I've spoken about my father, and about my friend (McKenzie) who's just written letters to her siblings and to me, the same letter, telling us what she wants for her funeral, what the passwords are for her bank account, her email accounts, that if something should happen to her...

She feels liberated now, untroubled. Liam says it's childish to fear death.

I say: "A fucked-up relationship with a parent keeps us children."

When an animal sends its cub into the wild, it's sending it to die. A child on its mother's breast knows nothing of death.

We spend three hours together, Liam and I, most of the time cocooned in that small room, a kind of laboratory. And that's the thing with these mini-relationships we have in these spaces – a beginning, a middle and an end in the span of two or three hours, sometimes less – as if we're being observed, as if there's some accelerated process we're part of in a controlled environment. As if there's something to learn from what we do, something that would benefit the rest of humanity, cure people of their ills and afflictions, elucidate some question the philosophers have been grappling with for centuries. We're the lab rats. If you were to regard us from above, a place like the sauna or the sex-club would look something like this:

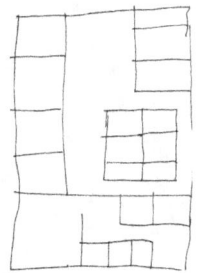

And that's the thing about those of us who have multiple sex partners, that's our gift, the ones who fuck around often... our way of seeing the world – our stories, the way we experience our beloveds – is unique, different to the lives of those who mate for life. One-night stands, afternoon-stands, they're our norm. A few hours contain an entire relationship: love and sex and intimacy reduced to its essence. We start off with the distillation. And then it's all we want, only beginnings, as if that's all there is, as if that's all we deserve, as if the bleeding of essence into extended time, the comfort and reassurance of that is not for us.

I cycled home singing. I cycled home and thought about getting this all down, writing about the hours Liam and I spent together and that we may never see each other again. He was not as beautiful in the light, and neither was I, perhaps, to him. But for those moments of closeness everything was good and kind and mindful. We were kind to each other, gentle and loving. In that box, naked, the two of us, all there was was life.

in Part 2

Will Mike bump into Martin at the sauna again? Will he get back with Marc when he visits him in Paris? And what about Hanif, and the masseur who offers "extras"? What will become of McKenzie and her gallery-owner lover? And Zaid? Has he got a bigger part to play?

write to Mike at
mike@theconfessionsofasexaddict.com